New Netherland Settlers

Captain Adriaen Crijnen Post & Claartje Moockers

By Lorine McGinnis Schulze

ISBN: 978-1-987938-20-3

Cover Image: Seal of New Netherland

The Seal of New Netherland created in 1623 displays a beaver with the legend SIGILLVM NOVI BELGII (The Seal of New Netherland). The crown at the summit represents the colony's royal Dutch source, while the rampant beaver on the empty field indicates the colony's activity of fur trading. The surrounding necklace of shells is wampum, symbol of the colony's wealth.

DEDICATION

This book is dedicated to my father Cecil Norman McGinnis.

Without the past we cannot build a future.

Table of Contents

ADRIAEN CRIJNEN POST & CLARA (CLAARTJE) MOOCKERS

Adriaen Crijnen Post may have been from The Hague, Netherlands. He and his wife Clara, aka Claartje, Moockers are first documented in the Church Registers in Recife Brazil in 1646. We might assign an approximate year of birth for Adriaen based on his likely marriage to Clara circa 1645. Since the Dutch generally married around the age of 25 we can make an educated theory that Adriaen was likely born circa 1620-1625. I have been unable to find such early records for births or marriages in the Hague for the time period needed.

Children baptised in Recife Brazil were:

1646. possibly Albert [1]
1647. Cornelis [2]
1649. Maria [3]

Recife, in the province of Pernambuco Brazil, started its existence at the mouth of the Capibaribe and Beberibe rivers in 1548 as a fishing settlement, but it soon grew and became the seat of government during the period when the Dutch occupied the North East region of Brazil.

Frustrated at not having found gold in Brazil the Portuguese began farming sugar cane in order to make colonization economically viable.

During the colonial period most of the sugar mills were concentrated in the North East region of Brazil and in 1535 the town of Olinda in Pernambuco was founded.

The wealth of the Brazilian North East was envied by the Dutch who invaded Pernambuco in 1630 and captured Olinda that same year. But the town was not easily defensible, and the Dutch soon burned and abandoned it, moving their settlement to the neighbouring marshes around the hamlet of Recife.

After the formation of the West India Company in 1621 the Dutch set their eyes on *Salvador da Bahia de Todos os Santos*, the most important town in Portuguese Brazil. The expedition for the conquest of Salvador da Bahia started in December 1623. The Dutch fleet arrived off Salvador in May 1624. They were joined by the Dutch troops who entered the town two days later. The Portuguese governor surrendered but the conquest was short lived. In April 1625, a Portuguese fleet sailed to Salvador and entered the town. On 30 April 1625, the Dutch capitulated.

The second attempt began in the summer of 1629. This time the Dutch objective was Pernambuco, the sought-after sugar colony in Brazil.

The commander of the Dutch fleet arrived at Pernambuco on February 1630. By the next evening the Dutch were in possession of Olinda, only a few miles from Recife. By the first week of March Portuguese resistance was over and the Dutch were masters of Recife, Olinda and the island of Antonio Vaz.

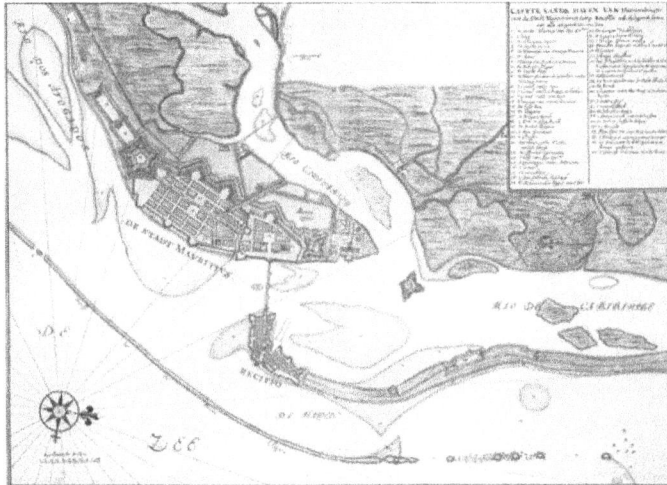

Mauritsstad and Recife 1643

The Portuguese governor Mathias de Albuquerque immediately organized a resistance. Some fortified camps were built around Recife, the most important one only about three miles from the town. For the next few years the Dutch and Portuguese attempts to capture each other's towns and forts continued.

At the beginning of 1636, reinforced by 2500 men from Portugal, the Portuguese again attacked. They advanced on Porto Calvo but its Dutch commander evacuated the town. The conquest of Porto Calvo gave the Portuguese the possibility to carry out many raids against Pernambuco that made settlement unsafe for the Dutch.

The Dutch subjects in Brazil were divided into two categories. The first were those employed by the WIC (soldiers, bureaucrats, Calvinist ministers). The second group was settlers, merchants, artisans, and tavern keepers. Many of these were ex-soldiers who had married and settled down but there were also settlers who had emigrated from the Netherlands to seek a new life in Nieuw Holland. The total white civilian population was about 3000.

The Dutch control on Brazil was always tenuous, and the WIC failed in its aim of colonization. The Dutch continued to lose their settlements and by the end of 1645 they possessed only Recife and the nearby Forts of Cabedello (Paraibá) and Ceulen (Rio Grande do Norte), as well as the islands of Itamaracá and Fernando de Noronha.

In November 1646 Fort Maurits was reoccupied by the Dutch but the following April the fort was abandoned. In February 1647 a Dutch expedition occupied the island of Itaparica in the Bay of Todos os Santos. In December 1647 the Dutch evacuated Itaparica. A new Dutch fleet under Witte de With left Holland the day after Christmas 1647 and arrived at Recife in March 1648.

In April 1648 a Dutch squadron of 5000 men under Commander Von Schoppe attacked the Portuguese forces and achieved some success. However the next day the Portuguese with only 2200 men launched an attack at the Guararapes that was an overwhelming victory. Soon the Portuguese reoccupied Olinda.

The Dutch at Recife were again besieged. At the end of 1648 the Dutch forces in Brazil totaled about 6000 white men and 600 Amerindians. In February 1649 a Dutch force of 3500 men occupied the Guararapes. The Portuguese marched against them with a force of 2600 men and the subsequent battle was an overwhelming victory for the Portuguese.

In February 1650 the situation of the Dutch at Recife, closely besieged by land, was very precarious, and the 3000 man garrison was demoralized. There were about 8000 civilians, of which roughly 3400 were the group made up of settlers, merchants, artisans, and tavern keepers, 600 were Jewish and 3000 to 4000 were Amerindians or blacks. The shortage of food and provisions was the worst enemy. The strength of the garrisons of Nieuw Holland was about 4000 men.

On 20 December 1653 a Portuguese fleet of 77 ships appeared off Recife. The depots of the town were full of provisions but the garrison was unprepared to offer resistance. Just one month later, on 22 January 1654 the Dutch asked for terms of surrender, and on 26 January the capitulation was signed. Not only Recife but all territories still in Dutch hands were included. The Portuguese made their triumphal entry into Recife on 28 January 1654. [4]

The Dutch were given three months in which either to depart or to embrace the Roman Catholic religion and become Portuguese citizens. In April 1654, a fleet of sixteen Dutch ships sat at anchor in the Harbour of Recife ready to evacuate the Dutch Protestants together with a small number of Dutch and Portuguese Jews.

Fifteen of the ships arrived safely in the Netherlands, however, the sixteenth was captured by Spanish pirates only to be overtaken by the St. Charles, a French privateer. After much negotiating, the master of the St. Charles agreed to bring a group of twenty-three Jewish men, women and children from the captured ship to New Amsterdam for 900 guilders in advance and 1,600 on arrival.

In September 1654, the French ship St. Charles arrived in New Amsterdam with 23 Jews who had fled from Brazil.

Origins of New Netherland

On September 19, 1609, the East India Company ship *Halve Maen (Half Moon)*, commanded by Henry Hudson, an Englishman working for Dutch businessmen who were seeking a passage to the Orient, reached the present-day Albany area. He had started up the Hudson River just 8 days earlier, on September 11. As the *Half Moon* lay at anchor, Hudson could see an island lying between two rivers to his north. To the west was a vast, unexplored wooded land.

In 1613, four years after Henry Hudson explored the river that now bears his name, a Dutch ship called the *Tiger* left Holland en route for the same waters. Adriaen Block, the captain, was an enterprising Dutchman who had made two earlier visits to these waters. The market for furs in Europe was growing, and Block's earlier visits had convinced him that he could fill his ship with furs which he could sell in the Netherlands as coats and hats.

Two months after he left the Netherlands, Block passed through the narrows that guard the entrance to what is now New York Harbour. Within a few weeks he was anchored at the southern tip of modern-day Manhattan Island, his ship filled with beaver and otter pelts. Unfortunately for Block and his men, the *Tiger* caught fire and burned. Block and his crew were stranded thousands of miles from home. Over the long difficult winter, Block and his men built a new ship, a 44 foot sailing vessel they named the *Restless*.

Cutting down trees and using whatever tools they could salvage from the *Tiger*, the men completed the ship by the spring of 1614 and prepared to sail home. It was on this return voyage that Block and his men discovered Long Island Sound. Block sailed into a freshwater river he named Fresh River (present day Connecticut River) and then dropped anchor at a place he called Hoeck van de Visschers or Point of the Fishers (present day Montauk Point). Having sailed completely around the long island, he claimed it for the Netherlands.

On reaching the Netherlands, Block appeared before government officials. After hearing his story they named the area he had surveyed (from Chesapeake Bay to Cape Cod) *Nieuw Nederlandt* (New Netherland). The name *Nieuw Nederlandt* appeared for the first time on October 11, 1614 in a resolution of the States General of the United Provinces. A charter concerning trading licenses between New France and Virginia was issued to merchants to begin trading, and a settlement was planned for the island where Block had built the *Restless*.

The goal of this newly formed New Netherland Company was to sponsor voyages to the area between 40 and 45 degrees north latitude -- the middle of present-day New Jersey to the coast of Maine. This huge region now had a formal, European name.

It wasn't long before the Dutch started construction on a log fort on an island at the northernmost part of the Hudson River that was navigable for their ships. This was near present-day Albany. At about the same time, merchants in the Netherlands formed a second business entity for the purposes of exploiting their new fur-rich land. This was the Charter of the Dutch West India Company (commonly referred to as the WIC) which was chartered by the States General on 3 June 1621.

The West India Company was designed to stand strong against Spain's interests in the New World. It was empowered to create colonies, settle people, attack Spanish vessels, conduct trade and make treaties with the Indians. The Province of New Netherland fell under the broad monopoly of this company. The capital of New Netherland was to be established on Manhattan Island and called New Amsterdam.

After the 3 June 1621 Charter of the West India Company, Fort Orange was built. It was built as a redoubt, surrounded by a moat 18 feet wide, mounted with 2 heavy and 11 light cannon, and garrisoned by 10 to 12 men. Around this was clustered a tiny hamlet occupied by the factors and servants of the WIC, who claimed all rights to the entire Indian trade. Although the charter, stated in part that they were to "... .advance the peopling of those fruitful and unsettled parts", colonization was not encouraged.

The first interest of the Dutch in the Netherlands was the fur trade. Thus the New World represented a business opportunity. By 1624 Dutch traders were establishing the fort near Albany. English colonists were in Virginia and Plymouth, and England was claiming the northeastern Atlantic Coast. Both the English and the Dutch laid claim to Long Island, where the Dutch took hold of the western end, and later, the English settled on the eastern end.

To bolster their own land claims, the Dutch began to establish more settlements. They sent groups of Walloons (French-speaking refugees from Belgium) to New Netherland. The first group of Walloons arrived on *Niew Nederlandt* in 1624 when approximately 30 families arrived. By 1626, these groups had a stronghold on Manhattan Island.

Peter Minuit arrived in New Netherland aboard the *See Meeuw* on May 4, 1626 to become Director of the Colony. He purchased Manhattan from the local Indians for 60 guilders' worth of trade goods. He ordered that the settlement should be located on the southern portion of Manhattan Island.

The Schaghen letter is the earliest reference to this this purchase. Peter Schaghen, the author, was the representative of the States General in the Assembly of the Nineteen of the West India Company. In the late summer of 1626 he reported the arrival of the ship *Wapen van Amsterdam* (Arms of Amsterdam) from New Netherland. In his report to the directors of the West India Company he announced the purchase of Manhattan Island for the value of 60 guilders. The original of this document is held by the Rijksarchief in The Hague. A copy of the document along with the English translation follows:

Rcvd. 7 November 1626

High and Mighty Lords,
Yesterday the ship the Arms of Amsterdam arrived here. It sailed from New Netherland out of the River Mauritius on the 23d of September. They report that our people are in good spirit and live in peace. The women also have borne some children there. They have purchased the Island Manhattes from the Indians for the value of 60 guilders. It is 11,000 morgens in size [about 22,000 acres]. They had all their grain sowed by the middle of May, and reaped by the middle of August They sent samples of these summer grains: wheat, rye, barley, oats, buckwheat, canary seed, beans and flax. The cargo of the aforesaid ship is:
7246 Beaver skins
178½ Otter skins
675 Otter skins
48 Mink skins
36 Lynx skins
33 Minks
34 Weasel skins

Many oak timbers and nut wood. Herewith, High and Mighty Lords, be commended to the mercy of the Almighty,

Your High and Mightinesses' obedient, P.Schaghen

Soon a tiny community was built on the southern tip of Manhattan Island and called New Amsterdam by the Dutch. It was walled off to the north by a thick forest laced with Indian trails. Trees were cut down and small houses were erected. Dirt cart paths became streets. Windmills for making flour were built at the tops of creeks; sailing vessels lined new docksides. To the east, across what is today's East River, lay Long Island.

There was too much to be gained financially by not allowing further colonization. Eventually the Directors in Amsterdam were forced to find a remedy. On the 7th of June 1629, under the title of *Freedoms and Exemptions*, Patroons, those individuals authorized to establish plantations in Dutch New Netherland, were given freedom to bring colonists to New Netherland. Anyone who shipped 50 colonists to the New World at his own expense could buy land along the Hudson River. This man, called a Patroon, had complete jurisdiction and full trade privileges (excluding furs) in perpetuity for himself and his heirs. Thus a type of feudal system was begun in the New World.

The Directors in Holland rushed to avail themselves of the privileges; for the Charter offered them profit and gratification. WIC officials mainly wanted to make a fast profit and return home. They had the monopoly on the fur trade; so the Patroons had a slower rate of return from their initial investment, as well as losses from shipwrecks and Indian raids. By 1635 four of the five original Patroonships had failed, with the only remaining (and successful) one being Rensselaerswyck, run by Kiliaen van Rensselaer from the Netherlands.

The failure of the West India Company and the Patroons to fulfill the requirements of their charter with respect to colonization and encouragement of agriculture was so great that in 1638 the States-General was called on. The Directors were forced to proclaim free trade (including the all-important fur trade) and free lands to private persons under certain restrictions. This had the happy effect of stimulating immigration to New Netherland from the Netherlands. Willem Kieft arrived on board *De Haring* on March 28, 1638 to assume the directorship of New Netherland. One year later an enumeration of buildings erected for the West India Company on the Island of Manhattan, at Pavonia, The Bay, and Forts Orange, Nassau and Hope was completed.

Kieft's tenure from 1638 to 1647 was ruinous. As an administrator he was incompetent, and he did not accept any opposition.

By 1643 Kieft, in his lust for more land, had managed single-handedly to start a large-scale war, named the Kieft War. In 1643 war broke out across Manhattan and western Long Island that resulted in more than 1,000 Indian deaths, including a massacre in what is today Massapequa. Although several of Kieft's Officers objected to the plan to attack the starving and destitute refugees who had fled from their Mohawk enemies, Kieft insisted and on 23 February 1643 his men attacked with the resulting massacre leaving over 100 Indians dead. The results on the inhabitants of New Netherland was devastating as the remaining Indians quickly retaliated. Willem Kieft, recalled in disgrace to the Netherlands, was lost at sea on board the ill-fated *Princess* on his return trip in 1647. The Princess, carrying approximately 100 passengers, including Kieft, his next in command Cornelis Melyn, one of Kieft's most vocal opponents Domine Everardus Bogardus, and others, floundered off the coast of Wales and sank. Fewer than 20 men were saved; the rest, including Kieft and Bogardus, perished.

Of the earliest settlers, more than half were French speaking Walloons from what is now Belgium. Father Joque, a Jesuit missionary from New France (present day Quebec province) who was visiting the village in 1644 noted only ten thatched cottages. He also reported that there were four hundred people in New Amsterdam and 18 different languages.

Father Jogue wrote to his supervisors in France:

New Netherlands in 1644

By Rev. Isaac Jogues, S.J.

New Holland which the Dutch call in Latin Novum Belgium, in their own language Nieuw Nederland, that is to say, New Low Countries, is situated between Virginia and New England. The mouth of the river called by some Nassau river or the great North river (to distinguish it from another which they call the South river) and which in some maps that I have recently seen is also called, I think, River Maurice, is at 40°30'. Its channel is deep, for the largest ships that ascend to Manhattes Island, which is seven leagues in circuit, and on which there is a fort to serve as the commencement of a town to be built there and to be called New Amsterdam.

This fort which is at the point of the island about five or six leagues from the mouth, is called Fort Amsterdam; it has four regular bastions mounted with several pieces or artillery. All these bastions and the curtains were in 1643 but ramparts of earth, most of which had crumbled away, so that the fort could be entered on all sides. There were no ditches. There were sixty soldiers to garrison the said fort and another which they had built still further up against the incursions of the savages their enemies. They were beginning to face the gates and bastions with stone. Within this fort stood a pretty large church built of stone; the house of the Governor, whom they called Director General, quite neatly built of brick, the storehouses and barracks.

On this island of Manhate and in its environs there may well be four or five hundred men of different sects and nations; the Director General told me that there were persons there of eighteen different languages; they are scattered here and there on the river, above and below as the beauty and convenience of the spot invited each to settle, some mechanics however who ply their trades are ranged under the fort; all the others were exposed to the incursions of the natives, who in the year 1643, while I was there actually killed some two score Hollanders and burnt many houses and barns full of wheat.

The river, which is very straight and runs due north and south, is at least a league broad before the fort. Ships lie at anchor in a bay which forms the other side of the island and can be defended from the fort.

Shortly before I arrived there three large vessels of 300 tons each had come to load wheat; two had found cargoes, the third could not be loaded because the savages had burnt a part of their grain. These ships came from the West Indies where the West India Company usually keeps up seventeen ships of war.

No religion is publicly exercised but the Calvinist, and orders are to admit none but Calvinists, but this is not observed, for there are, besides Calvinists, in the Colony Catholics, English Puritans, Lutherans, Anabaptists, here called Muistes &c.

When any one comes to settle in the country, they lend him horses, cows &c, they give him provisions, all which he repays as soon as he is at ease, and as to the land he pays in to the West India Company after ten years the tenth of the produce which he reaps.

This country is bounded on the New England side by a river they call the Fresche river, which serves as a boundary between them and the English. The English however come very near to them, preferring to hold lands under the Dutch who ask nothing from them rather than to be dependant on English Lords who exact rents and would fain be absolute. On the other side southward towards Virginia, its limits are the river which they call the South river on which there is also a Dutch settlement, but the Swedes have at its mouth another extremely well provided with men and cannon. It is believed that these Swedes are maintained by some merchants of Amsterdam, who are not satisfied that the West India Company should alone enjoy all the commerce of these parts. It is near this river that a gold mine is reported to have been found.

See in the work of the Sieur de Laet of Antwerp the table and article on New Belgium as he sometimes calls it or the map; Nova Anglia, Novu Belgium et Virginia.

It is about fifty years since the Hollanders came to these parts. The fort was begun in the year 1615: they began to settle about twenty years ago and there is already some little commerce with Virginia and New England.

The first comers found lands fit for use, formerly cleared by the savages who previously had fields here. Those who came later have cleared in the woods, which are mostly of oak. The soil is good. Deer hunting is abundant in the fall. There are some houses built of stone; they make lime of oyster shells, great heaps of which are found here made formerly by the savages, who subsisted in part by this fishery.

The climate is very mild. Lying at 40 2/3 degrees; there are many European fruits, as apples, pears, cherries. I reached there in October, and found even then a considerable quantity of peaches.

Ascending the river to the 43d degree you find the second Dutch settlement, which the flux and reflux reaches but does not pass. Ships of a hundred and a hundred and twenty tons can ascend to it. There are two things in this settlement, which is called Renselaerswick, as if to say the colony of Renselaer, who is a rich Amsterdam merchant: 1st a wretched little fort called Ft Orange, built of logs with four or five pieces of cannon of Breteuil and as many swivels. This has been reserved and is maintained by the West Indis Company. This fort was formerly on an island in the river, it is now on the main land towards the Hiroquois, a little above the said island. 2ndly, a colonie sent here by this Renselaer, who is the Patroon. This colonie is composed of about a hundred persons, who resident in some 25 or 30 houses, built along the river, as each one found it most convenient. In the principal house resides the Patroon's agent, the minister has his apart, in which service is performed. There is also a kind of bailiff here whom they call Seneschal, who administers justice. All their houses are merely of boards and thatched. As yet there is no mason work, except in the chimneys. The forests furnishing many large pines, they make boards by means of their mills which they have for the purpose.

They found some pieces of ground all ready, which the savages had formerly prepared and in which they sow wheat and oats for beer and for their horses, of which they have a great stock. There is little land fit for tillage, being crowded by hills which are bad soil. This obliges them to be separated the one from the other, and they occupy already two or three leagues of country.

Trade is free to all, this gives the Indians all things cheap, each of the Hollanders outbidding his neighbor and being satisfied provided he can gain some little profit.

This settlement is not more than twenty leagues from the Agniehronons, who can be reached either by land or by water, as the river on which the Iroquois lie falls into that which passes by the Dutch; but there are many shallow rapids and a fall of a short half league where the canoe has to be carried.

There are many nations between the two Dutch settlements, which are about thirty German leagues apart, that is about 50 or 60 French leagues. The Loups, whom the Iroquois call Agotzogenens, are the nearest to Renselaerwick and Ft Orange. War breaking out some years ago between the Iroquois and the Loups, the Dutch joined the latter against the former, but four having been taken and burnt they made peace. Some nations near the sea having murdered some Hollanders of the most distant settlement, the Hollanders killed 150 Indians, men, women and children; the latter having killed at divers intervals 40 Dutchmen, burnt several houses and committed ravages, estimated at the time that I was there at 200,000 liv. (two hundred thousand livres) troops were raised in New England, and in the beginning of winter the grass being low and some snow on the ground they pursued them with six hundred men, keeping two hundred always on the move and constantly relieving each other, so that the Indians, pent up in a large island and finding it impossible to escape, on account of the women and children, were cut to pieces to the number of sixteen hundred, women and children included. This obliged the rest of the Indians to make peace, which still continues. This occurred in 1643 and 1644.

Three Rivers in New France,
August 3d, 1646.

On May 11, 1647 Petrus Stuyvesant arrived at Manhattan with the West India Company ships *Groote Gerrit* and *Princess Amalia* to assume his position as

Director General of New Netherland. This position included the colonies at Curaçao, Bonaire and Aruba. At the start of Stuyvesant's administration, the population of New Netherland was an estimated 1,000 to 8,000. There is no exact count of the population at that time and only rough estimates can be made. By 1664 it was 10,000.

When he first arrived, Stuyvesant realized that English settlers were spilling into Dutch areas, so in 1650 he negotiated a treaty in Hartford. This treaty drew a line that began near present-day Greenwich, Connecticut, and crossed Long Island, beginning just west of what is now Oyster Bay. West of this line was Dutch, east of it was English.

In the early 1650s, the Dutch and English began fighting in Europe over trade and naval supremacy. This tension spilled over to the New World, where by the mid-1660s the English were trying to oust the Dutch from New Netherland. Locally, there was a desire for more territory and the English were encroaching the Dutch borders.

In 1656 the WIC decided that *"all mechanics and farmers who can prove their ability to earn a living here [New Netherland] shall receive free passage for themselves, their wives, and children"* Colonists were granted as much land as they could cultivate, but without the privileges Patroons had formerly held. The result was an increase in population from an estimated 2,000 in 1648 to 10,000 in 1660. New Netherland changed during this time from a trading post to a colony.

List of Governors or Director-Generals of New Netherland

1624-1625 Cornelis Jacobsen May
1625-1626 Willem Verhulst
1626-1632 Peter Minuit
1632-1633 Sebastian Jansen Krol
1633-1638 Wouter Van Twiller
1638-1647 Willem Kieft
1647-1664 Peter Stuyvesant
Rensselaerswyck Beginnings

Rensselaerswyck was the name given to the large tract of land granted to the wealthy Dutchman and Patroon, Killiaen Van Rensselaer in 1632. It included all the land that surrounded the present-day city of Albany and was situated on both sides of the Hudson River. The colony of Rensselaerswyck and the West India Company officials had long been involved in disputes over jurisdiction of territory around the Fort. When the patroon of Rensselaerswyck claimed all land west of the Hudson River from Beeren Island to Moenemin's Castle (including Fort Orange) had been bought for him. The WIC claimed that the land around the Fort, which had been built six years prior to the patroonship, belonged to the WIC and was not included in the purchase of 1632.

Killiaen Van Rensselaer established a patroonship in the upper Hudson Valley in order to cultivate the land and mine the wilderness for farm and forest products that could be exported to Europe and sold. Before his death in 1643, he hired hundreds of willing pioneers from the Old World and sent them to Rensselaerswyck to be his tenants. These settlers consisted of farmers, artisans, tradesmen, and others who could support the new settlement. Most of Van Rensselaer's tenants settled within a few miles of Fort Orange.

On 10 April 1652, Director General Stuyvesant issued a proclamation. By this proclamation the main settlement of the Colony of Rensselaerswyck was removed from the jurisdiction of the patroon and created as an independent village called Beverwyck. Beverwyck later became Albany. The jurisdiction of the court included Fort Orange, Beverwyck, Schenectady, Kinderhook, Claverack, Coxsackie, Catskill and (until 1661) Esopus (present day Kingston). The Colony of Rensselaerswcyk was not included in this jurisdiction until 1665 when the two courts were ordered to combine. Rensselaerswyck was the only one of five original Patroonships which was successful.

What we call "passenger lists" were in reality account books of credits and debits for voyages. All such "passenger lists" for travel from The Netherlands to New Netherland between 1654 and 1664 are derived from information on the debit side of the West India Company Account Book. Thus the set of "passenger lists" that we have for the years 1654-1664 are from an account book showing who owed money when they arrived. The published lists draw only from the debit side; the credit side has not been published.

Typical fare for passage was 36 florins for each adult; half that for young children; and nothing for nursing infants. Names were not usually recorded except for the person owing the money. Thus we might see an entry such as "Cornelis Jacobszen van Beest, wife and two children ages 11 and 5" with an amount due beside the entry. The ages of children were given in order to determine the fee for passage.

A typical voyage from the Netherlands to New Netherland took between 7 and 8 weeks.

Many of the early shipping records from the West India Company have not survived, and we must use other records to determine who the early settlers were and when they arrived in the colony. One of these is the 1651 Oath of Fidelity to the Patroon in Rensselaerswyck.

We can also consult the notarial records held in Amsterdam, Netherlands. Approximately 10% of the total notarial records have been indexed, and they hold a wealth of information. Most early settlers to New Netherland entered into a contract with their employer (the Patroon or the WIC or an established settler with money) before leaving for the New World. Many of these contracts can be found in the Amsterdam Notarial Records and include details such as origin of the settler, contract period (2 to 6 years), wages and other agreed-upon details, and sometimes the name of the ship the settler was to sail on. Even if the name of the ship is not given, the date of the contract is usually a good indicator of the sailing date, as the contracts were entered into shortly before the settler sailed. A search of Jaap Jacobs' list of ships sailing from the Netherlands to the New World (and back) can often provide a strong circumstantial case for an individual's being on board a specific ship.

Religion

The established church in the United Netherlands was the Reformed Church. In 1628 the Dutch West India Company sent the Reverend Jonas Michaelius as the first ordained minister to New Netherland. However, even before the arrival of Michaelius, Sebastiaen Jansz Kroll had been sent over in 1624 as a comforter of the sick. Although he began his duties in New Amsterdam, he was soon sent to Fort Orange, arriving there in 1628. The comforters of the sick were required to read prayers every morning and evening, as well as before and after meals, to instruct and comfort the sick, to exhort those who required or requested exhortation, and to read chapters from the Bible and sermons of an ordained minister. The comforters were empowered to baptize and marry, but could not administer Holy Communion. A special form of service was prepared for them to read.

After a few months at Fort Orange, Comforter Krol returned to the Netherlands to obtain a minister for New Netherland. However the settlement was not considered large enough to warrant a minister, and Bastien Krol returned to New Netherland with power to baptize and marry, provided he used the liturgy of the church in his services. When Governor Peter Minuit arrived in 1626 to take charge of the colony, he ordered that the settlement should center about the southern portion of Manhattan Island. Soon after Peter Minuit's order, Comforter Krol left Fort Orange to become the first comforter at New Amsterdam.

In 1632 the *Patroon* Kiliaen van Rensselaer gave instructions that settlers in the Colony of Rensselaerswyck should come together every Sunday and on holidays to read passages and chapters from the Bible. Brant Peele van Niekerck was authorized by van Rensselaer to read from the Bible.

The church founded at Albany in 1640 was the only one north of Esopus with a permanent ministry - other than Schenectady. All babies were baptised and their names entered in the *Doop Boek*, but sadly Albany's records are scanty prior to 1684. Many are lost completely. The population of Fort Orange is not known in this early period, but it was small. The first church built in 1648 was 84x19 feet, and consisted of only nine benches for those attending services. This church was still in use until 1656.

It was not until 1642 that Dominie Johannes Megapolensis was hired to preach in Rensselaerswyck. There was no church building, and it is not known where he held services. In 1649 Dominie Megapolensis was called from Rensselaerwyck (Albany) to assume charge at Manhattan. For the next year, his son-in-law, Dominie Grasmeer, conducted the Albany area services.

The *Patroon's* trading house on the west side of the Hudson River, had been turned into a church in March 1648. The *dominie* was an ordained minister of the Dutch Reformed Church sent by the church leadership in the Netherlands to minister to the Albany congregation. Dominie Gideon Schaets arrived in the Colony in July 1652 and was minister until his death in 1694. Both *dominies* (ministers) and Deacons (lay leaders) staffed the church. The Deacons were prominent Albany businessmen and officials.

In June 1656 the cornerstone of the new Dutch Reformed Church was laid. There are no known surviving registers from the church at Beverwyck/Albany before 1684.

Albany Dutch Reformed Church.
Courtesy New York State Museum

List of Ministers at the Albany Dutch Reformed Church

Johannes Megapolensis, Jr. 1642-52
Gideon Schaets, 1652-1691
Godefridus Dellius, 1683-1699
Johannes Nucella, 1699-1700
Johannes Lydius, 1700-1710
Petrus Van Driessen, 1712-1738
Cornelis Van Schie, 1733-1744
Theodorus Frielinghuysen,1746-59
Eilardus Westerlo, 1760-1790
John Bassett, 1787-1804
John B. Johnson, 1796-1802

Native Indians did not use currency. Instead they collected oblong shells which they polished and cut into beads. The finished highly polished beads were often attached to clothing. They were used as necklaces, belts and frequently strung in rows. These lengths of shells called *wampum* were often given as gifts. All beads were made up of highly polished cylinders about 1/8 " diameter and ¼" long, drilled length-wise and strung on ropes of hemp or the tendons of animals. While the local area dictated what shells could be used, in general black beads came from the local clam, known as the *quahaug*; while white beads came from winkles or periwinkles.

Indian beads were known by a variety of names among the early colonists – wampum, wampom-peage, wampeage, peage (which referred to beads that were strung), and in some localities such as New Netherland, seawan or seawand. In general the Dutch called it *seawan* (which they used for all shelled money), the English wampum. For the Indians, *wampum* referred strictly to white beads. They called their black beads *suckaubock*. The colonists used what they considered the generic term of *wampum* to refer to both varieties.

In 1609 Hudson's men received strings of beads from local Indians. The first European to use these beads for barter was a Dutch fur trader named Jacob Eelckens. In 1622 Eelckens demanded a ransom for a Pequot *sachem* (chief) on Long Island. The *wampum* Eelckens was given brought him more furs in trade than conventional trade goods. Before long the West India Company, recognizing a good thing, had their agents purchase all the *wampum* they could and take it north to Fort Orange. There they used it to buy furs from the Mahicans. Almost overnight *wampum* was functioning like money.

When Dutch traders encountered *wampum* they adopted it as a money substitute. Although more convenient than commodity money several problems developed with the use of *wampum*. It had no intrinsic value, and anyone could collect some shells and produce their own currency. With no central minting operation the quality of these products was often substandard. Shopkeepers needed to keep a vigilant eye for inferior *wampum* but there was no legislation in place that allowed them to refuse poor quality beads. Further, the amount of *wampum* produced was unregulated, and this eventually caused an oversupply.

In New Netherland *wampum* was legislated at four beads to the *stiver*, which was the Dutch equivalent of the English penny. However, so many poor quality unstrung beads were put into circulation that in April 1641 a law was passed prohibiting the use of unpolished beads during the month of May. During that month these poorer beads would be accepted in payment of taxes but only if they were strung and then only at the discounted rate of six beads to the stiver. The problems continued, and in May 1650 an ordinance was passed prohibiting the use of loose *wampum*. This law also further discounted poorly made *wampum* that circulated on string, so that they traded at the rate of eight beads to the stiver. As more and more *wampum* flooded the market the value of all beads declined.

In 1661 Director General Stuyvesant addressed the colonists' concern over the steady inflation of *wampum*. Much of it was "unpierced and half-finished, made of stone, bone, glass, shells, horn, nay even of wood, and broken". Huge quantities of this inferior *wampum* was being dumped in the colony by the English with the result that wages and cost of goods rose. Stuyvesant ordered that all wampum used as money must first be strung, and its value was fixed at six white or 3 black beads per *stiver* for high quality trade *wampum*, and eight white or four black beads per *stiver* for inferior quality.

Seawant, or unstrung beads, which had been prohibited from daily commerce in 1650, was still used for tax payments. As late as 1693 commuters on the New York and Brooklyn ferry could pay with either two pence in silver or eight *stivers* in *wampum*. The last recorded exchange of *wampum* as money was in New York in 1701.

Patronymics

The most common Dutch naming custom was that of patronymics, or identification of an individual based on his/her father's name. For example, Jan Albertszen is named after his father, Albert. Albertszen means son of a man named Albert. The patronymic was formed by adding -se, -sen, -szen and –sz.

The patronymic ending for women was formed by adding –s, or -sdr. Women were sometimes recorded under their husband's name, thus forming a husband-o-nymic of sorts. For example, Maria Goosens (Maria, daughter of a man named Goosen) was sometimes recorded as Maria Jans (Jans being the feminine version of her husband Steven Janszen's patronymic).

An individual could also be known by his place of origin. For example, Cornelis Antoniszen was known in some records as 'van Breuckelen', meaning 'from Breuckelen' (Breuckelen being a town in the Netherlands). The place-origin name could be a nationality, as in the case of Albert Andriessen from Norway, originator of the Bradt and Vanderzee families. He is entered in many records as Albert Andriessen de Noorman, meaning Albert, son of Andries, the Norseman (Norwegian).

An individual might be known by a personal characteristic, for e.g. Vrooman means a wise man; Krom means bent or crippled; De Witt means the white one. Maria Goosens was called Lange Mary (tall Mary) and is found as such in several records of the day. A fascinating example is that of Pieter Adriaenszen (Peter, son of Adriaen) who was given the nickname of Soo Gemackelyck (so easy-going) but was also known as Pieter Van Waggelen/Van Woggelum from his place of origin. His children adopted the surnames Mackelyck and Woglom.

Sometimes an occupation became the surname. For example Smit meant a (black)Smith; Schenck was a cupbearer, Metsalaer was a mason, Cuyper was a barrelmaker.

An individual might be known by many different 'surnames' - and entered in official records under these different names, making the search difficult unless you're aware of the names in use. For e.g. Cornelis Antoniszen mentioned above was known, and written of, under the following names:

Cornelis Antoniszen
Cornelis Teuniszen (Teunis being the diminuitive of Antony)
Cornelis Antoniszen/Teuniszen van Breuckelen
Cornelis Antoniszen/Teuniszen Van Slicht (this is how he signed his name and was likely a hereditary family name based on an old place of origin)

Broer Cornelis (name given him by Mohawks and meaning "Brother Cornelis" in Dutch))

There were also differences over the generations. Albert's sons and daughters took the surname Bradt except for his son Storm, born on the Atlantic Ocean during the family's sailing to the New World. Storm adopted the surname Vanderzee (from the sea) and this is the name his descendants carry.

The Dutch were much slower in adopting surnames as we know them than the English. Patronymics ended, theoretically, some time around 1687 but not everyone followed the new guidelines.

You must also be aware of the diminutives of regular first names, because the patronymic might be formed from the normal name or its diminuitive. For e.g.:

Antonis	Theunis/Teunis
Matthys	Thys/Tice
Harmanus	Harman, Manus
Jacobus	Cobus
Nicolas	Claes
Denys	Nys
Bartolomeus	Bartol, Meese/Meus
Cornelis	Krelis, Kees

Recommended Reading:

Dutch Systems in Family Naming New York-New Jersey by Rosalie Fellows Bailey in Genealogical Publications of the NGS May 1954 No. 12
New Netherland Naming Systems and Customs by Kenn Stryker-Rodda

Debunking The Post Family Genealogy Myth

Let me debunk the myth of the Post family, and the completely erroneous 'lineage' published in The Genealogical Magazine of New Jersey, Vol. X, No. 1. January 1935, under the title *"The Post Families of New Jersey"* by Dirk P. De Young.
This article sets forth a completely unsourced and non-viable lineage for Adriaen Crijnen Post. Mr. Young did give more than one disclaimer in his article:

"it [the lineage presented] must be accepted with the usual reservations until documentary proof of the connection is forthcoming"

However, this disclaimer is widely overlooked by researchers, and the suggested lineage has been repeated and sent forth into the genealogical community for so many years that many Post researchers accept it without question.

Let's take a critical look at Mr. Young's theory:

He suggests that Adriaen Crijnen Post was the son of Pieter Adrian's [sic] Post who died in The Hague in 1637. The major flaw in this proposed father for Adriaen is the patronymic of Crijnen which is attached to Adriaen. If he were indeed the son of Peter his patronymic would be Pietersz. (or variations such as Pietersen, Pieterse). The second flaw is that the author presents no baptismal source to substantiate his proposal. I suspect Young simply found some promising POST names in The Hague area and tried to slot Adriaen into the family.

What we do know is that Adriaen Post, who may have been from The Hague, Netherlands, resided in Brazil in the West India Company's colony with his wife Clara (Claartje) Moockers. Their names are found in the baptism record for Adriaen's daughter Maria who was baptised in Recife Brazil in June 1649. At this baptism Adriaen's patronymic of Crijnen is recorded.

The author of the incorrect lineage, does, in his favour, state very clearly

"That Capt. Adrian Post was a son of Peter Adrian's [sic] Post who died in the Hague in 1637 is inferred only, from circumstances"

This disclaimer is unfortunately overlooked by many Post descendants who continue to use this flawed lineage as if it were fact. If we look at the author's 'circumstances' for inferring the fatherhood, there are 3 extremely weak arguments:

"Capt. Adrian Post must have been born about 1600"["What is his source and/or reasoning for assuming such an early birth year?"]

The most glaring flaw in Young's proposed genealogy is that of his suggested grandfather for Adriaen Crijnen Post. Young gives the line as:

"Adrian Pieter's son [sic] Post b. about 1500 as father of Pieter Adrian's son [sic] Post who died in The Hague 1637"

Some mental math will reveal that a man born in 1500 would be pushing the limits to have a son who died in 1637. Assuming an age of 50 for the birth of Adrian Pieter's son, that would make the supposed son, Pieter Adrianse 87 at his death. Yes it is possible (unlikely in my mind) - but Young gives no baptismal records to substantiate his claim.

I think the most revealing flaw (and this in itself should be enough to make the entire proposed genealogy suspect!) is Young's outline of Pieter Post, son of Gerrit, born circa1300. The next generation is given as

"_ Post. A generation *assumed*, particulars unknown" (starred word is mine and given for emphasis).

Then Young continues with a Pieter Post born about 1360-75 who he gives as the son of unknown Post. Without sources, it is all guesswork. Without sources it is simply bad genealogy and should be discarded as quickly as possible.

Captain Adriaen Post in New Netherland

By the time Brazil fell to the Portuguese in 1654, the Post family had left for the Netherlands. On 30 June 1650 the ship "New Netherland's Fortune" sailed, arriving in New Netherland on 19 December 1650. It is thought that Adriaen and his family were almost certainly on board this ship.

Passenger lists as we know them, were not kept for ships sailing out of Holland. All "passenger lists" for travel from The Netherlands to New Netherland 1654-1664 came from information on the debit side of the *West India Company Account Book*. They show who owed money when they arrived. This account book is found in New Netherland Colonial Mss, vol. 14, Book KK. Typical fare was 36 florins; half that for young children; and nothing for nursing infants.

These accounts were made from the records of the West India Company, by order of the English rulers after the confiscation of the Company's property in New Netherland, and as assets of or debts due the Company, and to be collected by the English. The list seems to stop with the Eendracht which arrived on 19 July 1664. The English took over in Sept 1664 so that may have been the last passenger ship to arrive before that date

Adriaen and his family were on Staten Island by 1655 or earlier. Adriaen was a representative of Baron Hendrick van der Capellen, the owner of one-third of Staten Island. As the superintendent of a group of twenty people who were to farm Staten Island, Adriaen set up a colony which flourished.

Children born to Adriaen and Clara while they were on Staten Island were:

circa 1651. Adriaen
circa 1654. Lysbeth

In the summer of 1655 the Peach Tree War began over Hendrick Van Dyke's shooting of a Native woman stealing peaches from his trees in his orchard in Manhattan. As a result, the settlements on the lower Hudson River and around New York were destroyed by Iroquois attackers. On 15 September 1655, the colony on Staten Island was burned to the ground by the Natives from Hackensack. Twenty-three people were killed and sixty-seven taken prisoner, among them Adriaen, his wife, five children, and two servants.

In October 1655, Adriaen was released by the Hackensack chief Penneckeck to bargain with Petrus Stuyvessant for the release of prisoners. Adriaen made the journey between Manhattan and the Native headquarters at Paulus Hook, New Jersey several times before an agreement was reached. Fifty-six captives were released in exchange for powder, lead, guns, blankets and wampum. Among those freed were Adrian's wife and children.

Returning to Staten Island Adrian was ordered by Van der Capellan to gather survivors and erect a fort. Trying to keep the group fed, he found a few cattle that the Natives had overlooked roaming in the woods. That winter Adrian and his family camped in the company of some soldiers in the burnt-out settlement. They butchered some of the cattle they had found and obtained milk from others. Stuyvessant recommended to Post that he and "his people" and cattle move to the stockade on Long Island but Adrian stayed.

By Spring of 1656 Adrian was ill and unable to perform his duties, so his wife Clara Moockers Post requested that someone else be appointed as van der Capellen's agent. In April of 1656 Clara petitioned Stuyvessant asking that the soldiers be allowed to stay, but Stuyvessant decided that since there were only 6 or 7 people on the island, a garrison was not required and they should all move to Long Island.

Minute of the Return of 14 Prisoners (Men, Women, and Children) by Pennekeck, Chief of Achkinkeshaky. Monday, the 18th of October 1655.

"Whereas the chief of the Indians of Achkinkeshaky by name Pennekeok, has sent yesterday the 17th October, with Captain Post, one of the prisoners, fourteen Dutch people, men, women and children, to the Honble Director-General as a token of his good heart and intention and said chief requested, that the Honble Director-General would show his kindheartedness by sending some powder and lead.
"The Director-General and Council finding the request of Pennekeck of importance and having considered the present situation of affairs, have resolved and concluded, to send him, as a reward and token of affection two Indians, taken prisoners by our people, although not of his nation, and to give him some powder and lead, hoping by these means to get the other Christians in a friendly manner and at the same time to inform him, that when all the Christian prisoners have been returned to us, he shall be rewarded courteously. Thus done in Council of the Honble Director-General and Council, date as above.
(signed) "P. Stuyvesant, LaMontagne, Cor. Van Tienhoven." [5]

Message of the Indians Sent with Some Prisoners and Answer Thereto. 21st October 1655.
"Some powder and lead for 28 of our prisoners having been brought over to the Indians by Adriaen Post and Claes Jansen Ruyter, accompanied by Pieter Wolphertsen, pursuant to the resolution of the 19th October, they return this day and bring the said 28 prisoners according to the promise made by the Indians; and report, that the Sachem Pennekeck had directed them to tell the Honble Director-General, that Claes Jansen de Ruyter must return again to-day and bring with him a quantity of goods, as powder, lead, duffels, guns, wampum, etc to ransom the prisoners, who were still among them, 20 to 24 persons, else he would go with them into the interior. It was resolved, to send the aforesaid persons over again and to ask

how much they would take for the whole batch of prisoners or for each single one. Date as above." [6]

Answer of the Indians to the Foregoing. 26th October 1655.

"To-day, the 20th of October, Captain Adriaen Post and Claes Jansen de Ruyter came over from Paulus Hook and reported, that they had had a conference there with the chief of Achkinkeshaky and his people and other savages of Mochgeychkonk. They declared on their word of honor to the Council and related, that the said chief Pennekeck had, in the name of the other savages, directed them to tell and request the Honble Director-General, that, if his Honor would be pleased to send him and his people 75 pounds of powder and 40 bars of lead in three kegs, either as ransom or as present, they would immediately surrender the 28 prisoners.

"The Honble Director-General and Council and the Burgomasters of this City having heard the report of the aforesaid persons and having further seriously considered the inconvenience of the captured Christians, whose imprisonment rather ties our hands, they have with common advice and consent resolved (however unwillingly), for the sake of the prisoners' preservation and in the hope to recover them and the balance of the prisoners, to give to the savages the demanded lead and powder as ransom for the captives, as no other means can at present be discovered to recover them, and the more so, as they are scattered here and there among the Indians in the distant interior and to prove to them our sincere good-will, it is resolved to send them as a present 25 pounds of powder and 10 staves of lead over and above the ransom. Date as above: present were the Noble Director-General, the Honble Lamontagne and the Honble Fiscal Tienhoven." [7]

1655. Oct. 18. Instructions. To capt. Adriaen Post to obtain the release of the Christians still in the hands of the Indians; release of a Wappingh, and of an Esopus or Waerinnewaugh Indian.

Instructions of the honorable lord director general and councilors of New Netherland given to Capt. Adriaen Post.

... dat Ihde ...
... den trecken van ...
hem te senden twee gevangen ...
hop wel met van sijn volck, ...
... crist en loot op hooft den ...
christenen ... braue ... ...
... te doen aenstaen, soo wanneer ...
gevangenen ons sijn behandicht ... ...
te sullen ... ontpuckeren, Aldus gedaen ter ...
vanden E: H: D: generael en Raaden, was ...
(was getekent) P: Stuyvesant Lamontagne, Cor: van
Tienhoven

Instructie vanden E: H: D: g...
en Raaden van N: Nederlant ge...
aen Capt: Adriaen Post

Alsoo gemelte Capt: Adriaen post ons op gistteren ...
van onse gevangene christenen heeft overgeweest hem door de ...
sackemaa permitteert ter hant gestelt met bijgevo...
... dende, dat hij dale in sijn goede hart en goede affec...
aenden D: generael getoondt, ende wederom dat D: g...
goede guns te en trou te soude verwachten in wat crijst ...
... loot ... op den voorss Capt: post gerittet ...
en gelast wort wederom over te gaen en den voorss ...
sackima ... nader hem te aenwoorden en te seggen ...

Dat wij permitteren onder anderen sackimaes die bij ...
sijn bedancken voor hare goet hart en affectie die ...
betoont hebben int wederstenden vande gevangnen die ...
onder hem waeren, ende dat wij in trecken van onse ...
goede affectie ende goet hart ... hem wedderom ...

...van ons goet hart...
om die wederom dock bij hem
...stellen en hijn beste doen dat wij de
...gen christen ofte kranckheit die onder haer
...te onder ander sackmaet hijn wederom moogen
...conden ——

Ten tweeden sal aen pennicheit seggen dat et
gijen getuijgick is bij ons voor gevangens iets te
geven, noch oock voor gevangens iets te nemen
maer die uijt den goet hart wederom te bieden
gelijck wij dit bedijt gevangens doen, en oock
wederom van haer verwachten maer dat et oock is
dc bij ons getuijgickelijck de Arme gevangens die
veel conden ende ongemack en schaeden geleeden
hebben wat te geven op dat die niet meer groot hijn
gelijck wij aen haer gevangens gedaen hebben, souden
daervan oock gijen Crijt noch loot voorde gevangens
die pennicheit op gijsteren ons gesouden hebben
maer souden alleenich den wijnich daeden overleten
pennicheit en andere. oversten in t ijcken van ons
goet hart en dat alleen om dat hij haer best te
souden doen bij de andere sackimaes om de andere
gevangens te Crijgen, en dat bij sonde seggen
waer onder andere gevangens hijn die wanneer die
wederen souden coomen ——

Doch wanneer wij onse andere gevangens wederom hebben
wij dan wel genegicht hijn in t ijcken van onse goede
affectie wenich Crijt en loot te geven aen de
sackimaes en alsdan wederom haer goet hart
en affectie in schenckigick sullen verwachten als
onse gevangens weder hebben.

graden dat Niemant van ...
soo lange tot stilstant is ...
tegeben met des de generaele ...
bij de anders niet en sal gehooren

Den Bildien sal aen ponickkerke segge
Blosser wanneer Denige gehant en van ...
datter geen volck op staert sijn als de uu ...
en wanneer hij gelaeten tot dat hij geen ...
Calesbackers made den sackima ofte over ...
den de generaele gelooven mae te en dat die brijse post
sullen beboden Aetien int fort Amsterdam ...
adi itsupra

Ao
19 5:

Tieet generael en Raeden van N: Nederlant present de
Hoongden dese Steede op dato te sinusteende Paer Presio...
van dato 11 deses aengaende Sigenture en van denige pass...
die met de gebreet leggende scheepen versoecken t...
sijnde booso int Gital Conformeren Paer als noch in
de voorst resolutie van met de gereet leggende schi...
geen passagilis te laeten gaen made dessive Bildt...
te houden tot het vertroeck vaut sepit N: Amsterdam
alsdan in Ladinge leggende en apparente binnen...
te voegde bij sien alle passagilis wat te behueveden en
gaen sullen de generael en Raeden te Vredielijcke
Aduis gedaen ter virgaddinge van de Generael...
gehouden int fort Amsterdam in N: Nederlant
itsupra (was getteeckent) P: Stuyvesant Lamontay...
Cornelis van Denhoven A Hard Antoni Oloff A Noon...

Whereas Capt. Adriaen Post brought over 13 to 14 of our prisoners yesterday who were delivered into his hands by *Sackmaa* Pennekech, for the following reasons that he was demonstrating his good faith and affection to the director general and would await again the director general's good faith and favor in some powder and lead. Whereupon the aforesaid Capt. Post is authorized and instructed to cross over again and to respond to the aforesaid sachem on our behalf and to say that we thank Pennekech and the other sachems, who are with him, for their good faith and affection that they have demonstrated by returning the prisoners who were in his hands, and that we offer and send to him as a token of our good faith and affection two Indian prisoners, whom, although they are not of his people, but rather the one being a Wappingh [9] and the other from Esopus, or Waerinnewangh, he, Pennekech, is to accept as a token of our good faith and affection in order to repatriate each with his own people and nation, and to do his best to see that we get back the captured Dutch or *Swanekes* [10] who are among them or among the other sachems.

Second, he shall say to Pennekech that it is neither our custom to give anything for prisoners nor to accept anything for prisoners, but to return them with the goodness of the heart, as we hereby do with both of these prisoners, and expect the same from them; however, that it is better and customary by us to give something to the poor prisoners who have suffered much cold and discomfort and injury, so that they harbor no ill will, as we have done to their prisoners. It was for this reason that we sent no powder or lead for the prisoners released by Pennekech yesterday, but send only a little to the chief Pennekech and the other chiefs in token of our good faith, and that only so that they do their best with the other sachems to gain the release of the other prisoners, and that he is to tell where the other prisoners are and when they are to return.

However, when our other prisoners have been returned, we shall then be inclined as a token of our affection to give the sachems some powder and lead, as we shall then expect them to demonstrate their good faith and affection by gifts when we return our prisoners.

Whereas many false stories are carried back and forth by Dutchmen, who cross over without being sent by us, he is to tell Pennekech and the other chiefs that we have forbidden anyone of our village to cross over as long as the truce is in effect, except for Capt. Post or those who carry this token [   ] made by the director general's hand, and that he is not to believe the others.

Fourth, he is to say to Penekech that we also have forbidden that any people be at the shore when he sends over envoys except for those sent by us, and when he sends envoys that he not send any bad people or ragamuffins but rather sachems or chiefs in whom the director general may have faith, and that they shall have freedom to come and go. Done at Fort Amsterdam in New Netherland, *ady ut supra*, the 18th of October 1655. [11]

In December 1655 Cornelia Schellinger sued Captain Post in New Amsterdam. Post requested the case by heard by a judge on Staten Island but his request was refused. Below are the records of the full case, heard on December 6th [12]

Cornelia Schellinger, pltf. v/s Andries Pos, deft. In case of arrest. Deft. appeals to his competent Judge on Staten Island. Denies he is arrested. The Court Messenger being heard thereon, declares that he has arrested and summoned here Capt. Pos on the part of Cornelia; and whereas it is in case of arrest, the Court decide, that deft. is amenable to this Bench, and consequently that the question must be tried before this Court. Thereupon pltf. complains of force and violence, suffered from deft. First that he detains her cattle and will not let these go, but kills them and delivers them to the Man of War: And that he also has alienated stone and other goods. Requests, that deft. shall show, by what authority he acts, and retains the property of the Honble. Lord Van der Capelle and disposes thereof. Deft. Pos says, he has order and authority from the Honble Lord vander Capelle and is not bound to shew it to pltf. Pltf. says, whereas deft. asserts, he has power and orders from the Honble Lord vander Capelle, that she has an obligation, which she exhibits to the Court for the sum of fl. 1500 with interest at 6 per cent. dated 16. August 1653, which he is also bound to satisfy, inasmuch as he seizes and alienates the cattle which by the aforesaid obligation are specially hypothecated therefor. Deft. maintains, that those, who signed the obligation, are bound to pay the same. Pltf. says, that after writings were passed by form of exchange for the aforesaid sum on the Hon'ble Lord vander Capelle, his Lordship would not pay it. Looking, therefore, to the mortgage on the effects of the Lord Van der Capelle, requests accordingly, that deft. be condemned to sequester the said monies or cattle, and not to alienate the same before she be satisfied, as the money belongs to her children and orphans. Parties being heard, the Court find by the aforesaid obligation, that the cattle and effects of the Honble Lord van der Capelle are specially mortgaged for the satisfaction of the same. They therefore, decide, that pltf. shall exhibit in Court on the next day of meeting the written answer of the Lord vander Capelle, on which the bill of exchange is drawn; in the meanwhile to summon the signers of the obligation for the same time, to shew by what power they have pledged the effects of the Honble Lord van der Capelle. In the interim, deft. Andries Pos is ordered not to alienate nor estrange the effects of Lord vander Capelle.

Cornelia Schellinger appears again in Court with Capt. Pos, demanding of said Pos delivery of her one cow, which he has not yet delivered, saying she has agreed with Pos, that he should have one third of the cattle, which he brought for her, and that he, Pos, for his share, killed a whole ox, and she cannot get her cow. Deft. acknowledges the same and promises to deliver the cow to the pltf., as soon as he has an opportunity, saying that it was not favorable weather. Offers in case the said cow has strayed away, to deliver another in its place. The Court orders that deft. shall deliver pltf's cow on the first fair wind and weather; if possible within the time of 8 days.

1656. Proccedings in a suit between Jacobus Schellinger and Adriaen Post
Date: February 22 1656

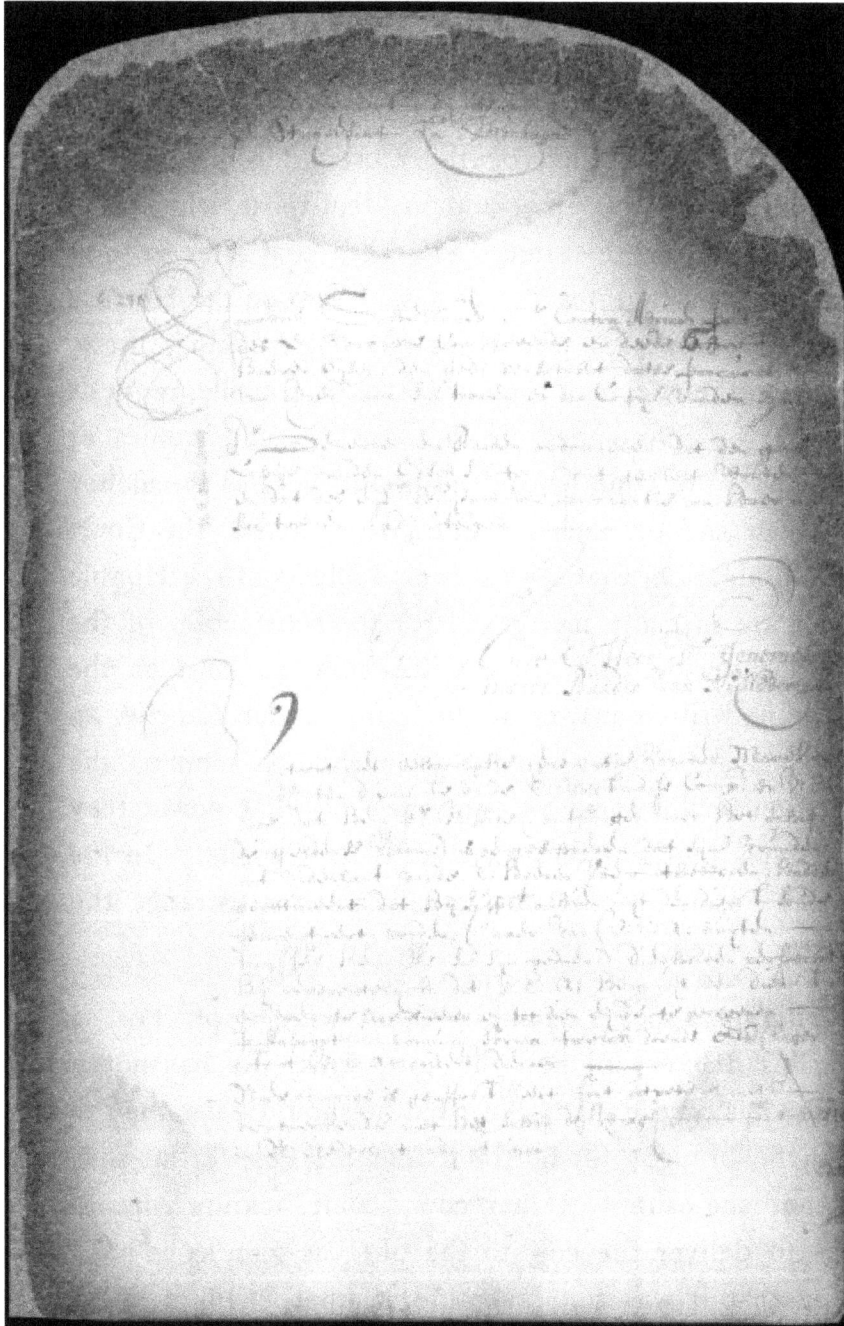

Jacobus Schellinger, plaintiff, against Adriaen Post, defendant; the plaintiff's wife appeared and submitted her charge in writing; the defendant requested that she show a power of attorney from her husband, and furnish a copy of the charge. The director general and councilors order that the defendant furnish a copy of the charge, and that the plaintiffs wife show a power of attorney from her husband. *Ady ut supra.* [13]

Proceedings. In the case of Jacob Schellinger vs. Adriaen Post, agent of baron van der Capelle, for payment of a note; continued.
Identifier: NYSA_A1809-78_V06_0311b
Date: February 29 1656

14

Jacob Schellinger, plaintiff, against Adriaen Post, defendant; the plaintiff's wife appears and requests payment of a promissory note signed by the attorney of the lord Van Capelle.

The defendant requests, before he answers, that she show a power of attorney from her husband, which she does.

The defendant, having seen the power of attorney, shows a letter of the lord Van Capelle, in which the aforesaid lord orders that the aforesaid promissory note be paid out of the leases received by Melijn.

The director general and councilors, having heard the parties, order the defendant to reply in writing to the written demand made by the plaintiff against him on the 25th of this month.

Order. Referring to arbitration a suit between Janneke Melyn vs. Adriaen Post, for cattle claimed by plaintiff.

Identifier: NYSA_A1809-78_V06_0352c

Date: April 4 1656

Janneken Melyns, plaintiff, against Adriaen Post, defendant; the plaintiff says that the defendant has illegally seized her livestock whereby she is suffering great damage and loss; she requests that he state why he has done such.

The defendant responds and request that she show power of attorney from her husband; he acknowledges to have from her seven head of livestock, which he does not refuse to return if she will pay the expenses incurred by him with regard to the aforesaid livestock.

The director general and councilors having heard the parties, refer the parties to *Sr.* Poulus Leendersen van de Grift and Pieter Wolphertsen van Couwenhoven, who are hereby authorized to settle completely by means of accommodation the dispute concerning the expenses incurred by the aforesaid livestock. If the parties are unable to agree, a third party shall be added to them. *Ady ut supra.*

Petition. Adriaen Post's wife, for a postponement of the suit between her husband, who is sick, and Jacob Schellinger, and that the soldiers may be allowed to remain for the present on Staten Island.
Identifier: NYSA_A1809-78_V06_0365a
Date: April 25 1656

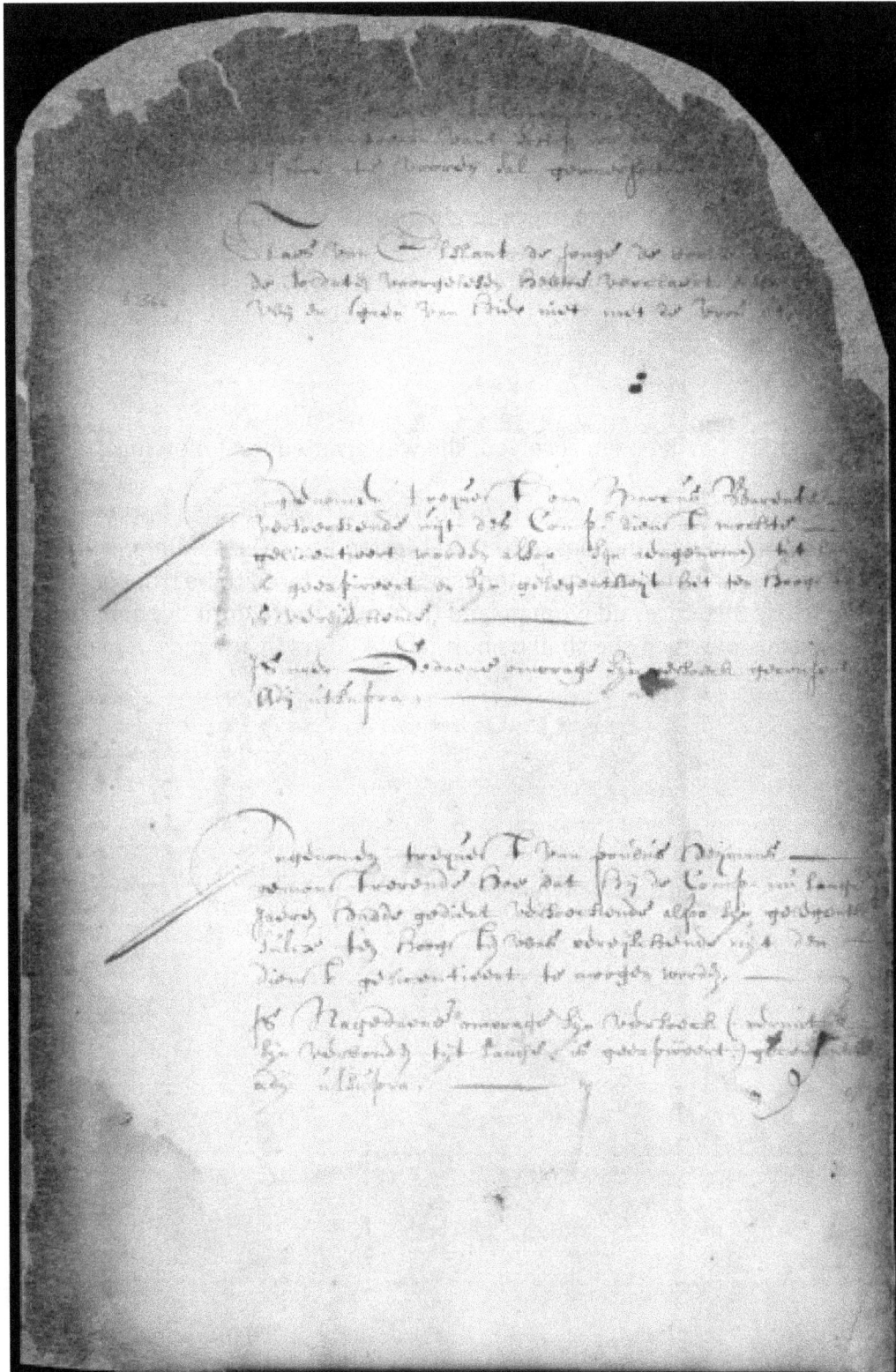

16

To the highly esteemed lords director general and councilors of New Netherland.
Highly esteemed lords.

Whereas Adriaen Post has fallen very ill on Staten Island, as is known to the soldiers arriving from the South River; therefore, his wife requests that the current court session may be continued in the case against Jacob Schellinger until the next opportunity. Also, whereas the soldiers stationed on Staten Island for security have to come back up here with Capt. Conincx' departure, it is also requested that your esteemed honors be pleased to act favorably upon the request of her husband, which was submitted thereon in the preceding month of March. So doing etc. [17]

Order. To the soldiers who accompanied Mdme. Post from Staten Island, to return thither with her.
Identifier: NYSA_A1809-78_V06_0365b
Date: April 25 1656

The foregoing petition having been received, she was granted the following decision:
Upon the request of the wife of Capt. Adriaen Post, it has been decided at the session of the director general and councilors of New Netherland that the soldiers, who came with the aforesaid woman from Staten Island, are ordered to be transported back to that place by the aforesaid woman, and to remain there until the departure of the ship *de Waagh*. of which she shall be notified 24 hours in advance. *Ady ut supra*. [18]

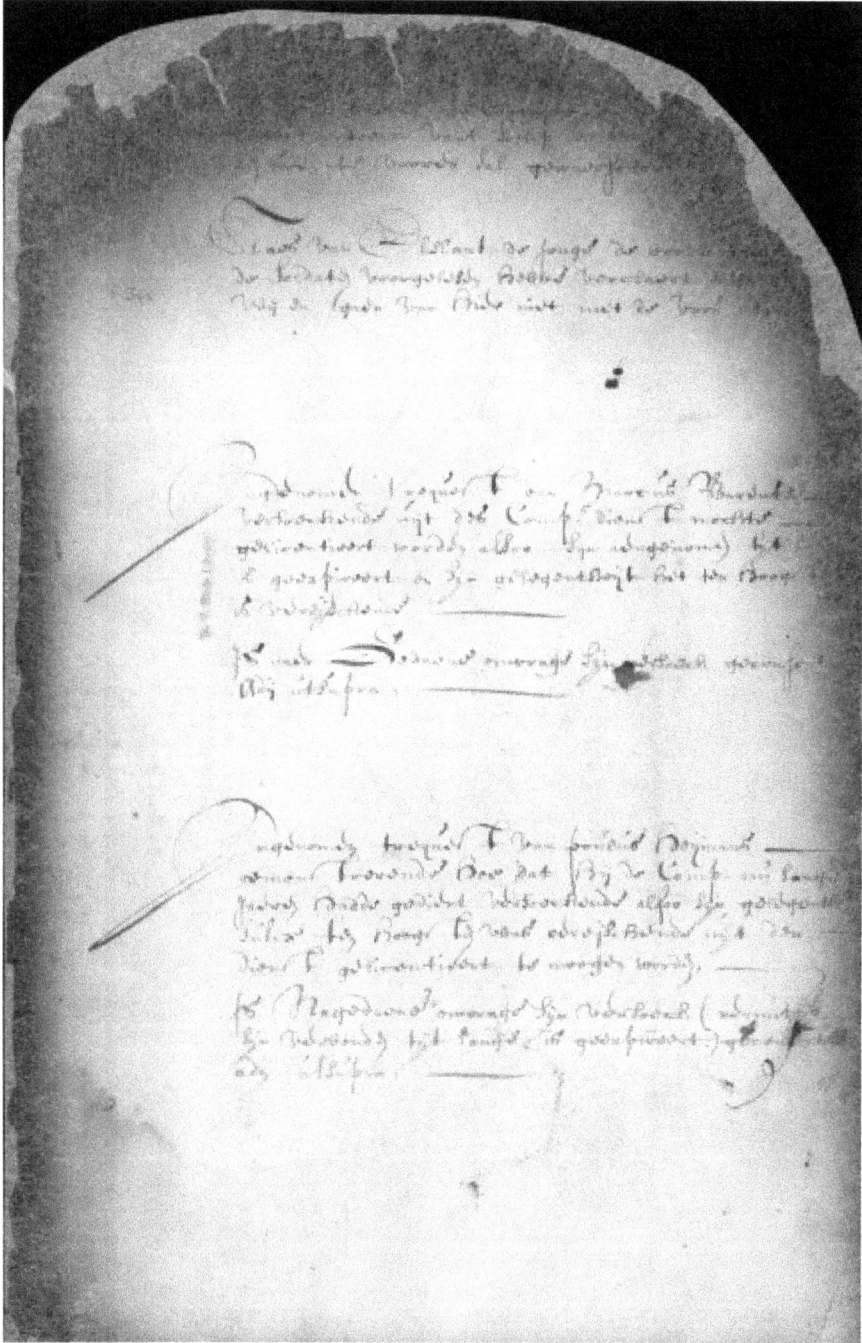

19

Return of service of Claes van Elsland, the court messenger, to the above order; the soldiers declared that they would not accompany the woman.
Identifier: NYSA_A1809-78_V06_0366a
Date: April 25 1656

Claes van Elslant *de Jong*e having read the foregoing order aloud to the soldiers, reports that they answered, "We will not leave this place with the woman." *Ady ut supra.*

Petition. Adriaen Post, agent of Mr. Van de Capelle, for an order to all his colonists to return to Staten Island, with answer thereto.
Identifier: NYSA_A1809-78_V08_0895b

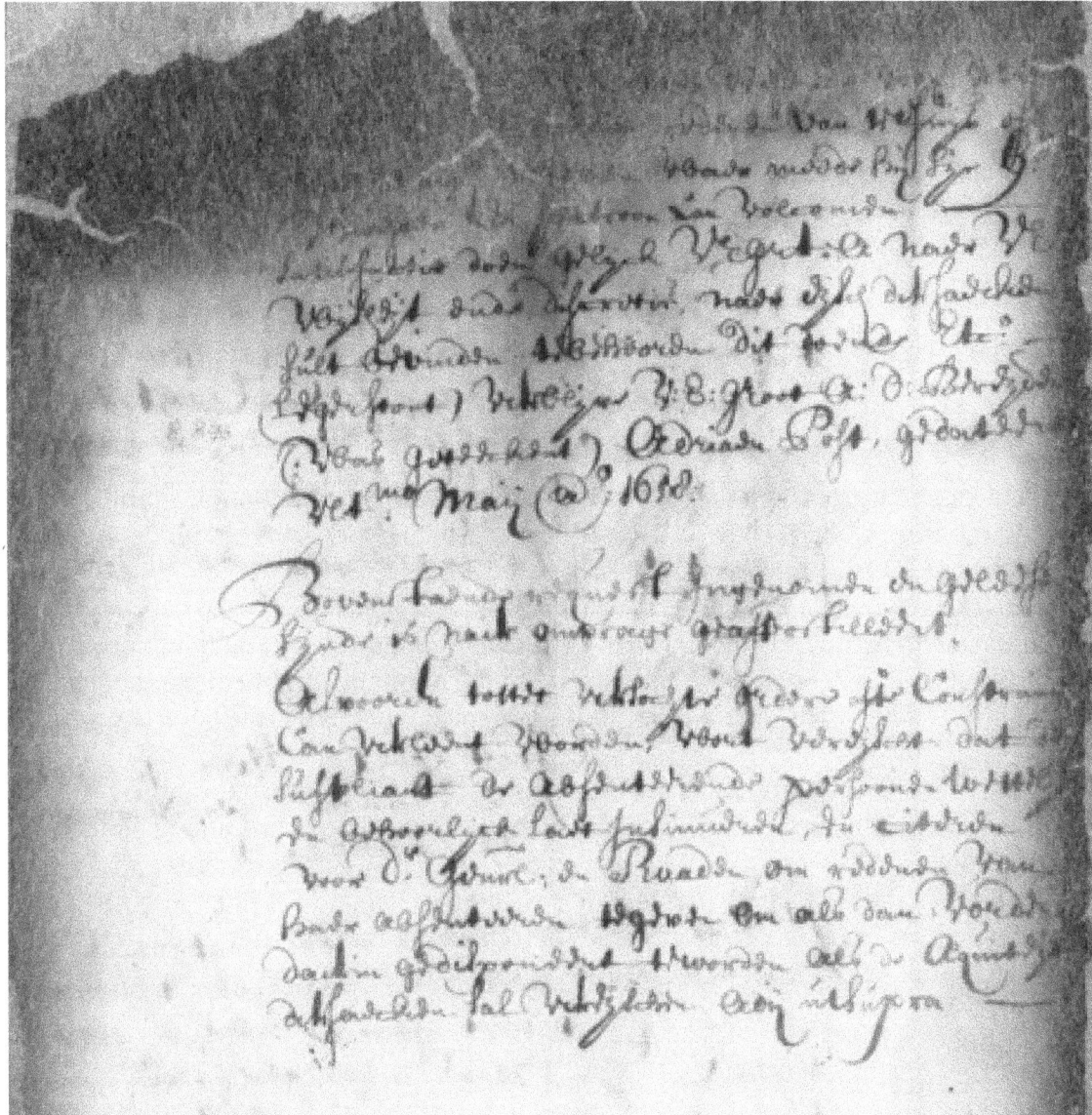

20

"List of yeomanry, men, women and children, men and maid servants, sent to New Netherland on Staten Island, since May, 1650; by Baron Hendrik van de Capelle tot Ryssel in the West Indies; and who survived that cruel and bloody destruction by the Indians, in September, 1655...

Capt. Adriaen Pos, with wife, five children, one servant, one girl; reside yet on the Island...

...In all 67 living souls. Recorded in this manner at Zutphen, on the 14th November, 1657, by the wife of Capt. Pos, and by the farmer Jan Aertsen van Heerde." *Alb. Rec. viii., 158.* [21]

From the above record we know that as of September 1655 Adriaen and Claartje had 5 living children. They were probably Albert, Cornelis, Maria, Adriaen and Lysbeth or if we use November 1657 as the date for referring to the 5 chldren, they would be Maria, Adriaen, probably Lysbeth, Margarita, and perhaps Cornelis or Albert.

Adrian regained his health and between 1657 and 1663 he and Clara baptised three more children at the Reformed Dutch Church in New Amsterdam. They were:

1657. Margarita [22]
1659. Francoys [23]
1663. Geertruyd [24]

Adriaen was in the New Amsterdam courts often, suing on behalf of his employer. We find mention of Adriaen in various court records in New Amsterdam between 1660 and 1663:

1660: Barent Cruytdop, plaintiff vs Capt. Post, defendant Plaintiff demands from defendentfl 29.7 in Zeawant. Defendentadmits the debt and says he never spoke to him about it til now. The W. court order defendentto pay the plaintiff. in six weeks. [25]

In November, 1661, Captain Post sued Laurenszen for "forty-one guilders, five stivers according to account." But Laurenszen's wife came forward and produced an offset account and "besides [p.248] this, some claim." The Burgomasters and Schepens referred the matter in question to Thomas Hall and Frerick Lubbersen to hear the parties, "to examine and decide their affairs, and if possible, reconcile them; if not, to report their decision to the Court. [26]

1662: Tryntje van Hengelen, plaintiff vs Adriaen Post, defendant Plaintiff, pursuant to the decision of the arbitrators in the case, which she had before this W. Court against Post, places in the hands of the W. Court the judgement of the arbitrators for the sum of fl. 14:10. Defendant says the costs are not with it; was ordered also to pay the costs, which he obeys. Plaintiff demands from defendant, in writing, the value of half an ox and cow, which he keeps from her, together with indemnity for damage to her grain according to valuation and estimate of the W. Court. Defendant demands copy of the demand. The W. Court order copy of the demand to be furnished to party thereunto to answer by the next Court day.

Tuesday 14 March 1662: Tryntie Van Hengelen, plaintiff vs Adriaan Post, defendant Defendant in default. Plaintiff requests that the defendant shall be ordered to answer the demand entered against him on 28 Feb. last. The W. Court orders Adriaan Post to answer on the next Court day the demand, which Tryntje van Hengelen has instituted against him.

1662: Adriaan Post answers the demand of Tryntje van Hengelen. The W. Court order copy to be furnished to party to reply thereunto at the next court day.

1662: Tryntje van Hengelen, plaintiff vs Adriaan Post, defendant Whereas parties dealy their suit entered against each other in writing before this W. Court, they were ordered to prosecute the same.

Tuesday 11 Dec. 1663 in the City Hall: Schepen Jacob Kip, arrestant and plaintiff vs Adriaan Post, arrested and defendant Plaintiff demands from defendant a balance according to a/c of 15 guilders in corn, and further as attorney of Albert Cornelis Wantenaar, the sume of 8 and 40 guilders 14 and a half stivers in seawant, demanding that the attachment shall stand good until he shall have paid him, with the interest of the demanded 15 guilders. Defendant admits the debt, promising to pay within the time of two or three weeks the 15 and 8 and 40 guilders and 14 and ahlf stivers. The W. Court condemn the defendant to satisfy and pay the plaintiff the sum demanded in his individual capacity and in his quality as attorney; declaring meanwhile the attachment so long valid. [27]

Captain Post eventually settled on the mainland of present-day Bergen, New Jersey.

Fourteen original settlers ofthe Haqueaqununck [Acquackononk] Tract in New Jersey were Hans Diedericks, Garret Garretsen, Walling Jacobs, Elias Michielsen, Hartman Michielsen, Johannes Michielsen, Adriaan Post, Urah Tomasen, Cornelis Roelofsen, Symon Jacobs, John Hendrick Speare, Cornelis Lubbers, and Abraham Bookey.

In March 28 of 1679 *"Captahem Peeters, the Native Sachem and Chief, in the prescence and by the aprobation of Memiseraen, Midnenas, Ghonnajea, Natives and Sachems of said Country, and in consideration of a certain parcel of Coates, Blanketts, kettles, Poweder, and other goodes"* conveyed the Tract known by the name of Haquequenunk unto Hans Diedericks, Garret Gareetsen, Waling Jacobs and Hendrick George.

On 22 November 1665, Adraien took the oath of allegiance to the King as an ensign in the Bergen Burgher Guard.
In May 1666 New Jersey governor Philip Carterett asked Adrian to be the interpreter at a meeting with the sachem Oraton to discuss a proposed land purchase.
In May 1671 he served on a jury at an Admiralty court at Elizabethtown.
On 7 June 1673 Adrian was elected one of Bergen's two representatives to the New Jersey General Assembly.
In 1675 he was made a Lieutenant in the Bergen Militia.
He was buried 18 February 1677 in the village of Bergen New Jersey and on April 7 his estate was adminstered

1677 April 7. Post, Captain Adrian, of Bergen. Administration on the estate of, granted to Cornelis Steenwyck of N. Y.

N. J. Archives, XXI., p. 40

28

Family Group Sheet for Adriaen Crijnen Post

Husband:		Adriaen Crijnen Post
	b:	Abt. 1620 in The Hague, Netherlands
	m:	Bef. 1646
	d:	Feb 1675/76 in Bergen, New Jersey; buried Old Bergen Churchyard
	Father:	
	Mother:	
	Other Spouses:	

Wife:		Claartje (Clara) Moockers
	b:	Bet. 1621-1626 in Netherlands
	Father:	Mr. Moockers
	Mother:	
	Other Spouses:	

Children:

1	Name:	Albert Post
M	b:	04 Nov 1646 in Recife, Pernambuco, Brazil
	Other Spouses:	

2	Name:	Cornelis Post
M	b:	1647 in Recife, Pernambuco, Brazil
	Other Spouses:	

3	Name:	Maria Post
F	b:	06 Jun 1649 in Recife, Pernambuco, Brazil
	m:	Abt. 1674 in New Amsterdam, New York, USA
	Spouse:	Jan Albertsen Bradt
	Other Spouses:	Eduwart Carbert(26 Nov 1699 in Albany New York USA)

4	Name:	Adrian Post
M	b:	Abt. 1651 in probably Staten Island, New York
	m:	17 Apr 1677 in Bergen New Jersey
	d:	Bef. Jun 1689 in Bergen, Sussex Co. New Jersey
	Spouse:	Catrintje Gerritse Van Wegenen
	Other Spouses:	

5	Name:	Lysbeth Post
F	b:	Abt. 1654 in probably Staten Island New York
	Other Spouses:	

6	Name:	Margarita Post
F	b:	06 Jun 1657 in New Amsterdam, New York
	m:	04 Dec 1675 in Kingston New York
	Spouse:	Johannes De Hooges
	Other Spouses:	

7	Name:	Francoys Post
M	b:	17 Mar 1658/59 in New Amsterdam, New York
	m:	22 Apr 1690 in Bergen New Jersey
	Spouse:	Martjis Jacobus
	Other Spouses:	Elena Van Schuyven(03 Jun 1721 in Hackensack, Bergen County, New Jersey)

8	Name:	Geertruyd Post
F	b:	21 Aug 1663 in New Amsterdam New York
	Other Spouses:	

Maria Post married Jan Albertse Bradt circa 1674 in New Netherland, possibly the Albany area. Jan was born circa 1648 in the Colony of Rensselaerswyck to the Norwegian settler Albert Andriessen de Noorman and wife Annatie Barents Van Rottmer.

Albert and Annatie were married in 1632 in Amsterdam. Albert was noted as 24 years old, from Fredrikstad Norway. Annatie is thought to have been from Otterndorf in Germany. Her mother Geesjie Barents assisted her at her marriage.

27-03-1632 - Andriess, Albert - Baerents, Annetje - DTB 438, p.289 - Huwelijksintekeningen van de KERK. - A24711000152

Between 1674 and 1690 Jan and Maria had 10 known children, the last six baptised in the Dutch Reformed Church in Albany. Those church records do not survive before 1684 so we have no record of the births of their first four known children - Adriaen, Antje, Clartje or Rebecca.

The children were: Adriaen, Antje, Clartje, Rebecca, Johannes, Pieter (died young), Andries, Barent, Pieter, and Storm.

Johannes. Feb. 3, 1684. Albany. Father Jan Albertsz Bratt. Presented by. Martje Elbertsz

Andries & Pieter (twins) Jan. 10, 1686 Albany. Father Jan Albertsz Bratt. Sp: Antoni Bratt. Presented by Annatje Bratt & Antje Cross.

Barent. Sept. 4, 1687. Albany. Father Jan Bratt. Witnesses Barent Albertz Bratt, Egbert ----. Presented by Susanna Jans

Pieter Nov. 11, 1688. Albany Reformed Church. Father Jan Bratt. Sp: Johannes Appel. Presented by – Apell

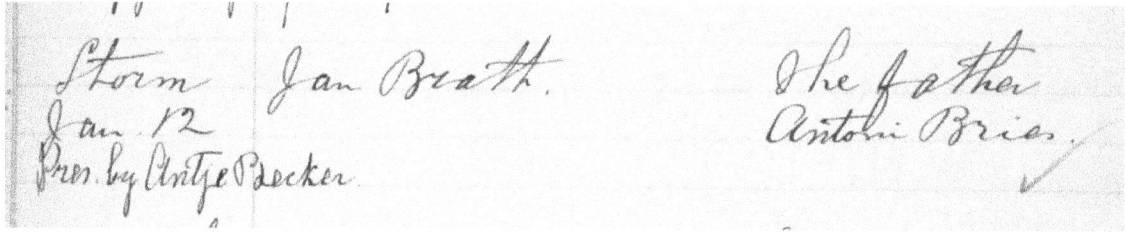

Storm. Jan 12, 1690. Albany. Father Jan Bratt. Sp. The father and Antoni Bries. Presented by Antje Becker

The last time Jan appears in the church records is May 23, 1697 when he sponsored the baptism of his grandaughter Maria. Maria was the daughter of Cornelis Van Slyk and Clara Bratt. Wit.: Jan Bratt, Dirk W. T. Broek, Geertruy Van Slyk. In the June 1697 census of Albany, Maria is listed as his widow.

Albany Census June 1697 shows Jan Bratts Widdow....................0 men-1 woman and 5 children. Her youngest still at home was Storm who would have been about 7 years old while the oldest still living at home was the twin Andries who was 12 years old.

On 26 November 1699 Maria Post Bradt married the Englishman Eduwart Carbert in Albany, Albany County, New York. [29]

Gen 2: Adriaen Post & Catrintje Gerritse Van Wegenen

On 17 April 1677 Adriaen Post married Catrintje Gerritse Van Wegenen in Bergen New Jersey. She was the daughter of Gerrit Gerritszen Van Wagenen & Annetje Hermanse. [30]

According to the History of the County of Hudson, New Jersey:

Gerrit Gerritsen and Annetje Hermansse were born and married at Wageningen, The Netherlands. Gerrit Gerritsen [Van Wagenen] had a document testifying to he and his wife's characters drawn up before they immigrated from Wageningen, Netherlands: "We, burgomasters, schepens and councilors of the city of Wagening, declare by these presents, that there appeared before us Hendrick Elissen and Jordiz Spiers, citizens of this city, at the request of Gerrit Gerritsen and Annetje Hermansse, his wife. They have testified and certified, as they do by these presents, that they have good knowledge of the above named Gerrit Gerritsen and Annetje Hermansse, his wife, as to their life and conversation, and that they have always been considered and esteemed as pious and honest people, and that no complaint of any evil or diorderly conduct has ever reached their ears; on the contrary, they have always led quiet, pious and honest lives, as it becomes pious and honest persons. They especially testify, that they govern their family well, and bring up their children in the fear of God, and in all modesty and respectability. As the above named persons have resolved to remove and proceed to New Netherland, in order to find greater convenience, they give this attestation, grounded on their knowledge of them, having known them intimately, and having been in contiuual intercourse with them for many years, living in the same neighborhood. In testimony of the truth, we the burgomasters of the city, have caused the private seal of the city to be hereto affixed. Done at Wageningen, 27th November, 1660; by the ordinance of the same J Aquelin." [31]

The family immigrated aboard De Trouw (Faith) when it sailed from Amsterdam December 1660 and arrived New Amsterdam before May 1661. They are recorded as "Gerrit Gerritsen, from Wageningen, and Wife and one child" [32]

Between 1677 and 1689, 7 children were born to this couple: Adriaen, Gerrit, Claartje, a stillborn son, Annetie (died young), Pieter, and Johannes. Adriaen died before his youngest son was baptised in June 1689.

On July 12, 1691 Catryna Gerrits, widow of Adriaan Post, living in Achquechnonk, married Gerrit Steynmets, widower of Vrouwtje Claes, living at Hasymus. Certifcate received 31 July 1691.

1678. 2 April; Adriaen Pos, Catharina Gerrits; Adriaen; Gerrit Gerritszen, Annetie Harmens

1680 26 Jan; Adriaen Pos, Catharina Gerrits; Gerrit; Jeuriaen Thomaszen, Jannetie Gerrits

1681. 4 Dec; Adraen Pos, Catharina Gerrits; Claertie; Gerrit Gerritszen de Jonge, Niefje Pieters

1684. 2 April; a son, died unbaptised

1685 6 May; Adriaen Post, Catharina Gerrits; Annetie; Frans Post, Fytie Gerrits [RDC, New York]

1688. 2 April. Pieter. Adriaen Post & Cathareyna Gerrits. Sp: Cornelis van Voorst with Aeltje Gerrits, young woman

Adriaen Post + Catharyna Gerrits
have their child baptised named
Pieter witnesses Cornelis van Voorst
with Aeltje Gerrits – young woman

1690. 10 June. Johannes. Catryna Gerrits, widow of Adriaen Post. Sp: Hermanus Gerritse, Cristoffel Steynmetz & Catryna Michielse, the wife of Walingh Jacobs

Johannes, Catryna Gerrits widow of Adriaen Post
10th June witnesses Hermanus Gerritse, Cristoffel Steynmetz, & Catryna Michielse the wife of Walingh Jacobs

On 04 December 1675 Margarita married Johannes De Hooges in Kingston New York. [33] He was the son of Antony De Hooges and Aefje Albertsen Bradt. Aefje was the sister of Jan Albertse Bradt who married Margarita's sister Maria Post.

Antony de Hooges was the business manager of Rensselaerswijck between March 1645 to March 1648. De Hooges recorded the colony's business and some personal observations in his Memorandum Book which has been translated and published online. [34]

Their children were:

Eva De Hooges born ca 1677
Clartje De Hooges baptised 27 April 1679 [35]
Annetie De Hooges baptised 19 November 1682 [36]
Anthony De Hooges baptised 12 October 1684 [37]
Catherina De Hooges baptised 14 February 1686 [38]
Marytie De Hooges born ca 1688
Johanna De Hooges baptised 31 August 1690 [39]

From the History of the City of Paterson and the County of Passaic:

It is probable that Francoys was an early settler at Acquackanonk. In 1695 he was chosen deacon of the church, and elder in 1699, 1705, 1711, 1716. He appears to have been a man of substance, for on April 4, 1696, Hans Dedrickes, of the town of Bergen, conveyed to "ffrancis Post of the township of Aqueckenonge," consideration £31 5s., current money of New Jersey, a "certaine parcell of Land Lyeing and being in the township of Aqueckenong . . . betwixt Adrian Post, and Jurian Thomas being of the hundred [acre] Lotts and is Numbered Two, together with the full and Absolute Right and privileges of the halfe of the fourteenth part of the comoniage, according to the whole of the purchase of Aquakenonge." Two years later, April 26, 1698, Cornelius Lubberts, of Bergen, for £30, conveys to "Franss Post of ye town of Achquikanuncque," "a certain lot or parcel of Land Containing one hundred acres lying within ye Pattent of Aquckononque above said being ye whole breadth of lott No. 10 & half ye breadth of ye No. 9 together with ye eight & twentieth part of ye rights of commons of ye sd town of Aquechkonunque according to aggrement made by ye Patentees to parties of said Patent wth its rights titles privileges & appurtenances unto said parcel of Land belonging or in any manner or way appertaining." This deed was acknowledged before Enoch Michaelse, Esq. These two deeds gave Post an equal fourteenth part of the undivided lands of Acquackanonk. In 1711 (November 27), he with seven others bought 2,800 acres, of land on Stony Road.

On 29 April 1690 Frans married Maeyke Cobes (Jacobes) in Bergen Dutch Reformed Church. [40] Their children were baptised in Bergen New Jersey:

Adrian Post baptised 29 March 1692

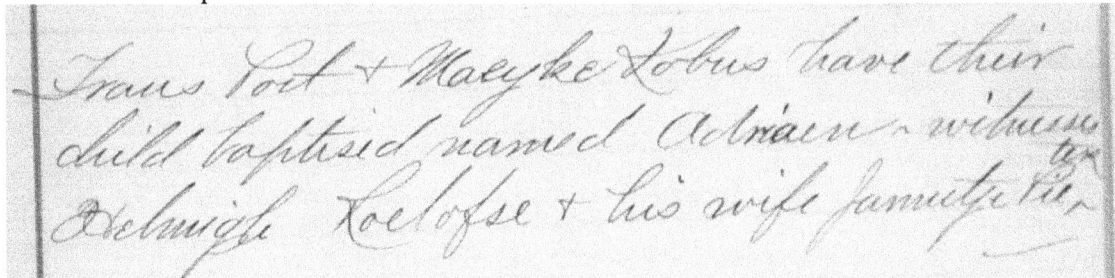

Jacobus Post born ca 1694
Johannes Post born ca 1696
Hendrick Post born ca 1698

After Maeyke's death, Francoys married Elena van Schuyven 03 June 1721 at Hackensack New Jersey. [41] No children are known to be born to this couple.

[1] C.J. Wasch, Doopregister der Hollanders in Brazilie 1633-1654 (Name: 1889;), 4 Nov. 1646 Adriaan _____ - Albert [more research required to determine if this is a child of Adriaen Crijnen].

[2] C.J. Wasch, Doopregister der Hollanders in Brazilie 1633-1654 (Name: 1889;), Adrian Crijnen - Cornelis. 1647. Sp. Dhr. Cornelis van den Brande, Geertruyt de Moucheron.

[3] C.J. Wasch, Doopregister der Hollanders in Brazilie 1633-1654 (Name: 1889;), Adriaen Crijnen Post, Clara Moockers. Wt Christoffel ---, Andelijina Caron, Dorothea Montanier.

[4] Marco Ramerini. The Dutch in Brazil: The WIC and a new Holland in South America. http://www.geocities.com/Athens/Styx/6497/brazil.html

[5] http://www.boydhouse.com/michelle/dehooges/adriaenpost.html

[6] http://www.boydhouse.com/michelle/dehooges/adriaenpost.html

[7] http://www.boydhouse.com/michelle/dehooges/adriaenpost.html

[8] New York State Archives. New Netherland. Council. Dutch colonial council minutes, 1638-1665. Series A1809. Volume 6.

[9] A member of the Wappingers, a Munsee group in Dutchess County

[10] A Delaware Indian word meaning "salty people," inferring that Europeans were white as salt

[11] Translation: Gehring, C., trans./ed., New York Historical Manuscripts: Dutch, Vol. 6, Council Minutes, 1655-1656 (Syracuse: 1995).

[12] Records of New Amsterdam, V. 1 pp 412, 413

[13] Translation: Gehring, C., trans./ed., New York Historical Manuscripts: Dutch, Vol. 6, Council Minutes, 1655-1656 (Syracuse: 1995).

[14] New York State Archives. New Netherland. Council. Dutch colonial council minutes, 1638-1665. Series A1809. Volume 6.

[15] New York State Archives. New Netherland. Council. Dutch colonial council minutes, 1638-1665. Series A1809. Volume 6

[16] New York State Archives. New Netherland. Council. Dutch colonial council minutes, 1638-1665. Series A18

[17] Translation: Gehring, C., trans./ed., New York Historical Manuscripts: Dutch, Vol. 6, Council Minutes, 1655-1656 (Syracuse: 1995)

[18] Translation: Gehring, C., trans./ed., New York Historical Manuscripts: Dutch, Vol. 6, Council Minutes, 1655-1656 (Syracuse: 1995).

[19] New York State Archives. New Netherland. Council. Dutch colonial council minutes, 1638-1665. Series A1809. Volume 6.

[20] New York State Archives. New Netherland. Council. Dutch colonial council minutes, 1638-1665. Series A1809. Volume 8.

[21] O'Callaghan, E. B., *The History of New Netherland, or New York under the Dutch*, Vol. II, NY: D. Appleton & Co., 1855, p. 291.

[22] 6 June 1657. Records of the Reformed Dutch Chuch in New York. Capt. Adriaen Post; Margarita; Pieter Tenneman, Cornelia Van Buuren. http://www.olivetreegenealogy.com/nn/church/rdcbapt4.shtml

[23] 17 Mar. Adriaen Post-Capt.; Francoys; Dirck Van Scheluynen, Jannetje Steynmutsen http://www.olivetreegenealogy.com/nn/church/rdcbapt4.shtml

[24] 21 Aug; Adriaen Post, Clara; Geertruyd; Nicolaes Booth, Fytie Michiels http://www.olivetreegenealogy.com/nn/church/rdcbapt5.shtml

[25] The Records of New Amsterdam From 1653 to 1674 edited by Berthold Fernow V. 3 p145

[26] Scandinavian Immigrants in New York 1630-1674. Part II: Danish Immigrants in New York 1630-1674

[27] The Records of New Amsterdam from 1653 to 1674 edited by Berhold Fernow. V. 4 p339

[28] New Jersey, Abstract of Wills, 1670-1817. Volume XXIII, Abstracts of Wills, 1670-1730

[29] The Holland Society, Marriage Record Albany Reformed Church, 1683-1804, Eduwart Carbert, y.m. b. England, living Albany & Maria Post, widow of Jan Brat, b. Brazil, living Albany.

[30] Adriaan Post, ym, from the Hague & Catryna Gerrits, yd, from Wageninge in Gelderland. Born ca 1657 in Wageningen, Gelderland.

[31] Charles H. (Charles Hardenburg) Winfield :: History of the county of Hudson, New Jersey : from its earliest settlement to the present time (Volume 1)

[32] http://www.olivetreegenealogy.com/ships/nnship32.shtml

[33] Baptismal and marriage registers of the old Dutch church of Kingston, Ulster County, New York by Kingston, N.Y. Reformed Dutch church. Hoes, Roswell Randall, 1850-1921. Johannes De Hooges, j.m. [young man] and Margarita Post, j.d. [young daughter] Banns recorded 17 November with consent of his father and mother, and consent of her father. Married after three lawful publications in the church

[34] New Netherland Institute. https://www.newnetherlandinstitute.org/research/online-publications/the-memorandum-book-of-antony-de-hooges/

[35] Baptismal and marriage registers of the old Dutch church of Kingston, Ulster County, New York by Kingston, N.Y. Reformed Dutch church. Hoes, Roswell Randall, 1850-1921. Johannes De Hoges [sic] Margriet Post. Claertie. Sp: Roeloff Swartout. Warnaer Hoornbeeck. Eva Alberts

[36] Baptismal and marriage registers of the old Dutch church of Kingston, Ulster County, New York by Kingston, N.Y. Reformed Dutch church. Hoes, Roswell Randall, 1850-1921. Johannes De Hooges (wife not named) Geertie (crossed out and Annetie inserted). Sp: none named

[37] Baptismal and marriage registers of the old Dutch church of Kingston, Ulster County, New York by Kingston, N.Y. Reformed Dutch church. Hoes, Roswell Randall, 1850-1921. Johannes d'Hooges [sic] Margrita Post. Antoni. Sp: Roeloff Swartwout. Willem Montaigne. Eva Alberts. Cathrina de Hooges

[38] Baptismal and marriage registers of the old Dutch church of Kingston, Ulster County, New York by Kingston, N.Y. Reformed Dutch church. Hoes, Roswell Randall, 1850-1921. Johannes De Hooges, Margriet Post. Cathrina. Sp: Gerrit Cornelisz. Chieltie Cornelisz.

[39] Baptismal and marriage registers of the old Dutch church of Kingston, Ulster County, New York by Kingston, N.Y. Reformed Dutch church. Hoes, Roswell Randall, 1850-1921. Johannes De Hooges. (wife's name not mentioned). Johanna. Sp: Elizabeth Gardenier. Roeloff Swartout. Antoni Bries

[40] Dingman Versteeg and Thomas E. Vermilye, Bergen Records: Records of the Reformed Protestant Dutch Church of Bergen in NJ 1666-1788. Post, Frans & Maeyke Cobus with certificate from Achqueknonk

[41] U.S., Dutch Reformed Church Records in Selected States, 1639-1989. New Jersey. Hackensack NJ, Book 62. Were registered for marriage Frans Post widower of Maeyke Jacobes, with Elna Van Schuyven, Y.D. [single woman] born at Acquiggenonck, both living there

www.ingramcontent.com/pod-product-compliance
Lightning Source LLC
Chambersburg PA
CBHW080245270326
41926CB00020B/4377